THE SECRET
JUNG

Swati Singh is a research scholar living in Gurgaon in India, working on Rudyard Kipling and colonial discourse at the University of Rajasthan. The idea for writing this book came up via a chance meeting on the Jaipur-Delhi train, and realising in conversation with a fellow passenger how Kipling still excites interest.

The Secret History
of the Jungle Book:
How Mowgli could save the world

Swati Singh

THE REAL PRESS

www.therealpress.co.uk

Published in 2016 by the Real Press,
www.therealpress.co.uk © Swati Singh

The moral right of Swati Singh to be identified as the
author of this work has been asserted in accordance with
the Copyright, Designs and Patents Acts of 1988.

ISBN (print) 9780993523915
ISBN (epub) 9780993523922

To my father, my first teacher.

Chapters

Foreword

Human beings are born story tellers. It is the
ability to articulate oneself through a commonly
evolved speech pattern that distinguishes mankind
from all other animals. Stories too have their own
way of just happening to you on their own. One
never knows when, on a particular day and in a
seemingly innocuous moment, a story just
happens.

This story began in India, on a railway platform
with two strangers from two parts of the world,
each going her own way, who found themselves in
the same coach – and sharing the same berth in a
railway carriage – discussing an author who
happened to connect their worlds.

It was on a Jaipur-Delhi train that East met
West and they got along discussing their different
worlds, only to discover that their worlds were not
so different after all. East and West, it seemed,
were reconciled and at peace finally— forgiving
and accepting of the excesses of the past. The
author who provided these two worlds with a

common ground to talk on was none other than Rudyard Kipling — an Indian born writer of British origins, and one of the greatest storytellers of all times.

And here we are again, discussing Kipling and his amazing story of childhood fantasy in an Indian jungle.

Chapter 1
Between the lines

The year 2015 marked 150 years of Kipling, and also 120 years of Kipling's *The Jungle Book (*1894) and its sequel *The Second Jungle Book* (1895). The 'Jungle Book' series is primarily remembered by all of us for the antics of the wolf child Mowgli and other characters of the jungle immortalized by Walt Disney in the animated version of the books. *The Jungle Book.*

This is particularly so of Mowgli, who continues to excite interest and interpretation even today, so much so that the latest animated Mowgli in a new avatar hits screen on the 15 April 2016.

Kipling wrote *The Jungle Book* series in Brattleboro, Vermont, in the USA, oceans away from the land and the people he was writing about. But any reader of the Jungle Books would be struck with wonder to see the vivid imagination with which Kipling brings alive the flora and fauna, as also the vernacular dialects of Indian speech. Kipling's description of the Indian spring in the story *Spring Running* from *The Second*

Jungle Book is one of the finest representations of the Indian climate and landscape by any writer. Kipling's pictorial and sensuous description of the Indian Spring goes as follows:

> "In an Indian Jungle, the seasons slide one into the other almost without division... Spring is the most wonderful because she has not to cover a clean, bare field with new leaves and flowers, but to drive before her and to put away the hanging-on, over-surviving raffle of half-green things which the gentle winter has suffered to live, and to make the partly dressed stale earth feel new and young once more. And this she does so well that there is no spring in the world like the jungle spring".

The rhythm and intimacy of Kipling's description, the careful choice of words, gives to the beauty of this prose passage the grace and vitality of poetry. But the passage has been chosen to illustrate the deeply personal relationship that Kipling shared with the country of his birth, India.

The stories in *The Jungle Book* also follow a folk-tale like structure, more reminiscent of the Indian way of storytelling, with a moral hidden in each story, coming through innocuously to the reader. Critics have wondered if these stories take root in the fables and folklore that Kipling heard as a child from his Portuguese *ayah* and Hindu bearer as he remembered in his autobiography, *Something of Myself*. The fable like tone of the stories in *The Jungle Books* almost echoes the subconscious influence of the Indian folklore that Kipling must have heard time and again in his childhood.

For most of us, *The Jungle Book* remains an enduring memory of our childhoods. Kipling was weaving magic and fantasy when he wrote *The Jungle Books* years ago, dedicating them to his beloved daughter Josephine, who unfortunately died young. *The Jungle Books* took the world of letters with surprise and widespread admiration. Even the harshest critic of the 'imperialist' Kipling could not help but behold in wonder the magic that Kipling had weaved in Mowgli's story.

Later, *The Jungle Books* were read for the themes of imperialism and colonisation, but the early reception for them was largely positive and was also overwhelming. While *The Jungle Books* as a whole are a collection of numerous beast fables, it was mostly the Mowgli stories which caught the attention of the world.

In fact, Kipling wrote the Mowgli stories

backwards, which is to say that the character of Mowgli was first envisaged as a young man. The first Mowgli story was *In the Rukh*, a short story which appeared in the collection *Many Inventions,* published in 1893. It was from here that Kipling went back in time and imagined the wonderful life that the man-cub Mowgli must have lived as a child and the result was the Mowgli stories in *The Jungle Books*.

In his autobiography, *Something of Myself,* Kipling says: "After blocking out the main idea in my head, the pen took charge and I watched it begin to write stories about Mowgli and animals which later grew into *The Jungle Books*". With these comments, Kipling added to the magic and fascination that forms the world of *The Jungle Books*.

It is a curious fact that, even today, *The Jungle Books* in original, as well as in translations and adaptations, remain the first introduction to India for a large part of the world. Sam Miller, in his *A Strange Kind of Paradise: India through Foreign Eyes*, says: "An impressive case can be made for Kipling as a writer who invented the idea of India as a land of childhood, a place of innocence and wonder." Miller gives the experience of his own family as an example and says how it was Disney's

1967 animated *Jungle Book* movie video that caught his young son's attention and curiosity, just as the first film that his mother saw and loved was the 1942 live action *Jungle Book* movie by the Korda Brothers. With this candid admiration of Kipling, Miller puts in perspective the widespread popularity that *The Jungle Books* have enjoyed, and the kind of influence they have continued to exert down the years.

Kipling's *The Jungle Books* attracted the attention not only of critics and readers, but also of the Western screenplay writers, who saw in it a potential story exploring the 'exotic' East of popular imagination. They were not mistaken, because *The Jungle Book* indeed draws on the myths and fables of India where it is set and gives to it a unique perspective.

The first adaptation of *The Jungle Books* was done by the Hungarian Korda brothers who brought to movie screens in 1942 *Rudyard Kipling's Jungle Book in Technicolor*. This adaptation was a live action adventure and was told in the narrator's voice of *Buldeo*, the hunter of Kipling's book, to a visiting British *memsahib*. The narrative mostly focuses on Buldeo as he chases Mowgli through the forest. This adaptation took bits and parts from the first and the second *Jungle*

Books, mixing Mowgli's miraculous childhood among wolves with the story about the treasure guarded by an old white python which actually appeared in *The Second Jungle Book*, playing on all the available stereotypes of India as the land of wild beasts and fabulous treasures, while keeping close to the original Kipling story.

The real breakthrough in the history of screen adaptations of the *Jungle Books* came with the Walt Disney Animation Studio's 1967 cartoon film version of the same. It was the nineteenth feature in the Walt Disney Animated Classics series directed by Wolfgang Reitherman and the last film to be personally supervised by Walt Disney himself.

The film was a huge success and grossed over $73 million in the United States in its first release and as much again from two re-releases. In 1994, Disney released a live action remake of *The Jungle Book* starring Bruce Reitherman as Mowgli. Disney released a theatrical sequel to its first *Jungle Book* movie in 2003 as *The Jungle Book 2*. This sequel was **not** Kipling's *The Second Jungle Book*, but a continuation of the first Disney movie with a rather similar story line.

Disney is once again releasing a remake of the 1967 animated movie in a 3D live-action format with Jon Favreau as director and introduces the Indian origin child actor Neel Sethi as Mowgli. This movie releases on the 15 April 2016.

Warner Brother's production too has a *Jungle Book* movie in the pipelines titled *Jungle Book: Origins* set for release on 6 October 2017. The multiple remakes and adaptations point to the popularity as well as the unexplored potential for story telling inherent in *The Jungle Books*.

An interesting anecdote that is common trivia about the making of the 1967 animated *Jungle Book* movie by Disney is its initial conceptualisation by Bill Peet, one of the long-standing animators and screenplay writers associated with the Disney Studio who first thought of animating *The Jungle Book* into a movie. The screenplay that Peet gave to Walt Disney was too faithful to the original to be suitable for children's viewing.

After a very public spat, Disney rejected Bill Peet's script and got on board a new team of creative directors headed by Larry Clemmons. The story goes that Walt Disney handed this new team a copy each of *The Jungle Book* and said: "The first thing I want you to do is not to read it." The results were for the world to see in the musical that turned out in the form of *The Jungle Book* movie. The Disney team had tweaked the original characters as *Baloo, Bagheera, Hathi, Shere Khan* and *Kaa*. It also excluded a few like *Chil* the Kite and *Tabaqui* the jackal, while introducing new characters as *King Louis*, King of the Apes and the singing Vultures. The wolf pack which is integral to the original Mowgli story was also significantly missing in the movie.

Disney toned down the narrative of the original work by Kipling and loosely re-interpreted it as the musical Mowgli story that worked its magic on the big screen and onto the hearts of its viewers. But we have to remember that the Disney movie came with its own baggage of racial implications with the introduction of the ape King Louis, who was widely perceived as an offensive representation of Afro-Americans. The dancing ape was widely perceived as a racialized caricature of jazz culture artists.

A major difference in the book and its screen version was the interchanging of the roles of *Baloo* and *Bagheera*. While, in the book, Baloo is the wise teacher of the Jungle Laws and Bagheera is a playful character, an elder brother figure to the young Mowgli, in the Disney movie the roles are totally reversed. The movie also changes the python *Kaa* to a secondary antagonist in the movie who is after Mowgli's life, while in the original book Kaa is the nemesis of the monkey folk whom he hypnotises before eating, with his peculiar dance, rather than through his eyes. Every jungle animal in the book is supposed to fall under the spell of Kaa's dance, except Mowgli, who finds it amusing and stays unaffected.

The Disney movie is brilliant in conception but is, to say the least, irreverent to the Kipling book. The Zen like calm and serious teacher of the jungle laws, Baloo, is transformed in the movie to a bumbling, clumsy foolish old bear, "a stupid jungle bum", who goes fooling around the jungle, seeking just the 'simple bare necessities' of life.

Bagheera on the other hand is made a kind of godfather to Mowgli who finds him floating downstream in a basket and rescues him, giving him to a family of wolves who just had cubs, to be raised amongst them. In Mowgli's growing years, Bagheera is always around, watching over his protégée, until he decides it is the right time to send him back to the man village where he actually belongs to. It is when Bagheera takes the unsuspecting Mowgli towards the man village, and tells him on way about where they are going, that a petulant Mowgli decides to run away from Bagheera back into the jungle which has been his home.

It is on his lone adventure through the jungle that Mowgli meets *Kaa*, the hypnotising python, who almost kills him, *Hathi* and his regiment, Baloo the bear, the monkeys and their leader King Louis and finally the nemesis that he has been told of, *Shere Khan* himself. The climax sees the fight between Shere Khan and Mowgli. Mowgli, helped by Baloo and the vultures, succeeds in driving Shere Khan away from the jungle with the help of fire – gifted to him by the chance providence of a lightning fall on a dried tree stump which catches light.

Shere Khan is shamed into running away with his tail on fire, while Mowgli is reunited with his friends, Baloo and Bagheera. The end sees Mowgli lured to the man village by a song sung by a beautiful young girl fetching water from the stream, with a disappointed Baloo asking him to come back to the jungle while Bagheera bids him a happy farewell.

Disney's *The Jungle Book* movie remains a pleasure to watch even down the years, with its award winning music and world class animation. The animal characters are all quirky, with the exception of Shere Khan and Bagheera, while the jungle itself bursts with bright colours, beautiful flowers, and sunlight. Life in the Disney jungle is easy and fun where the man-cub Mowgli can be a wolf, a bear, a monkey or a marching elephant, as the occasion and his fantasy demand, with the occasional fear of a wily Kaa or a predatory Shere Khan.

While both Disney's conception of *The Jungle Book* adaptation, and even Kipling's conception of this magical fantasy where animals speak and boys grow up amongst wolves as playmates, may seem to be a happy coincidence of randomly selected beasts, there is a definite method to the madness that seems to abound in both the versions of the books.

Disney simply lifted the mythic-fantasy elements of Kipling's work and domesticated it by making Mowgli a lost infant who lands in some sort of a Biblical Eden. Disney's characterisation of Baloo, the brown bear, and Bagheera, the black panther, was a clever playing of the screen appearances that these characters took.

The singing vultures were an allusion to the Beatles and took their inspiration from them. The Beatles were even approached to sing the song of the vultures but they refused. Disney also played on the stereotype of the East by making the python Kaa, the secondary antagonist to Mowgli, along with Shere Khan, the tiger. The snake has always been symbolic of evil in western mythology and there was no way that the European imagination could think of a snake which was friendly to man.

And this takes us to Kipling's characterisation of the animals which peopled the jungle books. Kipling was thinking, not as a British or as an American when he cast Kaa as the friendly Python who would guide Mowgli in the ways of the Jungle and help him become its overlord. In *The Jungle Books* it is Kaa, more than Baloo or Bagheera, who helps Mowgli in the deciding moment to get the crucial victory over the red dogs that come to hound the jungle, which allows Mowgli to claim unchallenged authority over the jungle as its uncrowned lord.

Kipling's Indian background must have made him familiar with the snake charmers who used to abound in colonial India, when simple tricks as a dancing monkey and a terrifying snake hidden in the basket were common entertainment for the resident British children. This perhaps explains itself as the inspiration for Kaa's dance that hypnotises its prey into a trance before it is taken in deathly grip by the python.

Likewise, as a study of the senior Kipling's treatise on Indian beasts, *Beast and Man in India* shows, Kipling must have been familiar with the

Indian mythology of the creator of the world Vishnu, who rests in the coiled lap of the Hundred mouthed snake *Sheshnag*, a deity in his own respect and sacred to the Hindus. There are sequences in the stories of *The Second Jungle Book* which sees Mowgli frequently resting in the cushioned comfort of Kaa's coils. Kaa is a friend and mentor to Mowgli, the only creature of the Jungle who can claim a sort of comradeship with Mowgli, a familiarity that comes of mutual respect. Even Baloo and Bagheera, the teacher and protector of Mowgli, are moved to the shadows as Mowgli grows in stature so that he can even command Hathi to come to him, a thing unheard of in the jungle.

It is not difficult to understand that the secret to commanding Hathi is given to Mowgli by Kaa, the only creature of the jungle as old as Hathi himself, and who knows of all the hidden secrets of the jungle. In the same way, while the Disney movie gave Hathi a wife, *Winifred* and a family, and made him a funny commander who goes marching in the jungle as the jungle patrol with his family and prefers being called *Colonel Hathi*, Kipling's Hathi is worlds apart.

In Kipling's book, Hathi the elephant, is the descendant of *Tha*, first of Elephants, who created the jungle and all its creatures and gave to the jungle its code of conduct, and had three sons but no wife. Hathi, is the unacknowledged leader of the jungle, and a serious dignified stately creature who hardly speaks. The difference in the characterisation can once more be attributed to Kipling's knowledge of the myth of the elephant god *Ganesha*, widely revered in India as the harbinger of all good, the remover of obstacles and the foremost amongst all gods whose blessings must be invoked before any auspicious activity for its successful completion.

For a long time, Kipling was considered a Nazi supporter because his early manuscripts carried the symbol of the swastika, symbolic of *Ganesha* in Hindu mythology, which was used in its inverted form as a symbol of the Nazi regime in Germany.

Further in *The Jungle Book*, Kipling speaks ignominiously of the monkeys and specifies that they have no leader and therefore are an outcast jungle tribe with no memory and no rules governing their existence. The monkeys kidnap Mowgli in the *Jungle Book* because they want to know from him the secret of making shelter. On the other hand, in the Disney movie, the monkeys have a leader, King Louis, and the monkeys kidnap him because King Louis wants to get from Mowgli the secret of fire, something that Mowgli himself is unaware of.

While the Disney conception was a brilliant attempt at creating a fun loving, jiving, singing character, Kipling's conception of the monkeys, referred to in the book as the *Bandar-folk*, is rather more problematic. In *The Jungle Books*, Kipling is creating a sort of hierarchy of characters in which the monkeys are placed last. The monkeys are on the margin of the discourse that goes on in *The Jungle Books*. They are creatures on the fringes of the jungle society, apparently with no laws, no purpose, unclean and uncouth by nature. This will be somewhat contrary to expectations considering that monkeys are considered one of the most intelligent of all animals.

Without going into the rhetoric of Kipling's imperialist vision and his presentation of the monkeys as 'half-devil and half-child' of the imperialist ideas expressed in his now infamous poem *The White Man's Burden*, an alternative idea comes to the mind for which we have to go to Kipling's Indian past. In his autobiography, Kipling retells an anecdote when once as a young reporter he was bribed by a native raja of a state with a gift of an expensive cashmere shawl and a five hundred rupee note hidden in a basket of fruits, and how the nineteen-year-old Kipling returned the 'insult' in an 'Asaiatico' style by sending back the gift to the Raja, who was obviously a high caste, through the hands of the 'camp-sweeper' who was not.

A myth common amongst Indians in colonial times spoke of the British as the descendants of *Hanuman*, the monkey general of prince *Rama*, human incarnation of the *Lord Vishnu*. But in rather disrespectful terms, the British themselves were referred to occasionally as the 'monkey-army', both of which facts are chronicled by John Lockwood Kipling in the chapter titled 'Of Monkeys' in his book *Beast and Man in India*.

Moreover, the Hindu worship and adoration of monkeys as semi-deities is something that Kipling must have been aware of as a resident Anglo-Indian. One can't thus be very far from the truth in stating that his characterisation of the monkeys in *The Jungle Book*, in a complete reversal of their valorous narrative given in the great Hindu epic *Ramayana*, again something that Kipling must have been aware of, Kipling was perhaps returning once again in kind the insult, 'Asiatico' style, that had been levelled against 'his' nation, the British.

*

The climax that Disney gave to its movie version is quite different to the climax that Kipling gave to the conflict between Mowgli and Shere Khan. Unlike the movie, where Mowgli confronts Shere Khan head on and leaves him alive with the shame of a burning tail so that he goes into the jungle, the real Kipling story gives the gory details of how Mowgli plans for days, waiting for the right moment when he might attack Shere Khan.

Mowgli literally ambushes a sleeping Shere Khan before he is killed and then skins the tiger, fulfilling his promise to the wolf council. Shere Khan is no mean enemy to be handled alone and Mowgli kills him when he is resting after a full meal, with the help of *Akela*, the old leader of the wolf pack and *Gray Brother*, his own foster wolf brother, by trapping him between the bulls he grazes on the one side and cows on the other side.

Shere Khan is actually trampled to death by the pack of bulls that Mowgli drives towards him and is then skinned by Mowgli. Cunning and cruelty pave the way for Mowgli's return to the jungle. After Shere Khan's death, Mowgli returns to rule the wolf pack as their new leader, and spreads the tiger skin on the rock for a seat, and as a symbol of his sovereignty. In this new terrible form that Mowgli takes, subduing the jungle folk with the glare of his eyes, he takes the form of the Indian god *Shiva*, the destroyer, one who sits yogi-like on a mat of tiger skin, but whose calm demeanour hides the terrible power of his third eye, which when opened in anger burns to death whatever it looks upon. Even *Messua*, the woman who adopts Mowgli as her lost son, remarks he has a handsome face and eyes that burn like 'red fire'.

Although it is difficult to point out if Kipling was actually taking these elements of Indian mythology, the ideas do not seem farfetched when one realises that Kipling, through his own Indian years, as also through the legacy of his family who lived long in India, was definitely aware of these mythic Indian tales. Considering the strange ways in which the creative mind works, one never knows how and when something buried deep in the unconscious surfaces in the fictional characters one creates.

With Mowgli, one feels as if Kipling gave his imagination free flight, moulding him with that rapturous imagination which always leads to magic. Mowgli, as imagined on cinema screens, has been popularly seen as a dark, wild Indian boy, but Kipling describes Mowgli saying: "His voice was clear and bell-like, utterly different from the whine of the native, and his face as he lifted it in the sunshine might have been that of an angel strayed among the woods." It is as if, in Mowgli, Kipling envisioned a demi-god of the Indian woods.

Kipling's vision for Mowgli as a ruler of men and of animals is symbolically heralded in the sequence where the monkeys carry him away and *Chil* the kite hovers overhead. Kipling was here referring to the Indian myth that believes kites circling children's head are ominous of good fortune and ordain for them a future as king among men.

The Disney movie barely skims through the surface of Kipling's work. Even as an inspired work, it is only a loose inspiration. Kipling's *The Jungle Book* was a work way ahead of its time as children's literature. The dark, menacing undertones of the book and its rampant violence were not really meant for children. But again, Kipling as a child had seen that dark side of life against which normal children grow shielded, in the love and warmth of parental care. This was bound to reflect itself somewhere in his writings.

Kipling's tale of the feral man-cub Mowgli was not meant to be a story merely about a boy in the midst of talking animals, but a story about gritty survival in the face of all odds. Unlike Disney's Mowgli, Kipling's Mowgli had nobody but himself to help when Shere Khan lifted him from his village as an infant. It was on his own that the child somehow escaped the hungry tiger and found his way to the mother wolf *Raksha's* den. It was the innate fearlessness of his character that helped him thrive in the company of his wolf brothers.

The Mowgli stories in *The Jungle Book* are also about a man's perpetual quest of his identity and of his place in the world. Kipling did not see the Mowgli stories as merely the fantastic journey of a boy from child to man in the jungle, but more importantly as Mowgli's emotional journey as the passage from childhood to youth, and the realisation that he is not a wolf, as he had believed in all the years of his growing, but a man – a creature that he had all the while looked at from afar and with mistrust.

Kipling's Mowgli was not the caricature that Walt Disney presented in his *Jungle Book* movie, a child-man who willingly becomes whatever animal his fantasy pleases him to be, be it a bear or an elephant, but a real human being who thinks and yet cannot either fathom or reconcile the contraries which define his life. Mowgli was a wonder of the author's creation – part man and part beast. Fearless, free and independent, he easily brought the human and the animal worlds in a delightful contact, creating a sort of Eden on Earth. On the other hand, to the more mature and discerning of the Kipling readers, Mowgli was a puzzle, the kind of postmodern hero who constantly eludes a conclusive interpretation.

In Mowgli, Kipling gave perhaps the first modern hero of English literature, full of angst and doubts about his identity, caught between two worlds and belonging to neither.

The grown up Mowgli has to undergo real pain as he realises that, apart from his foster wolf-family and the original beasts of the jungle who had accepted him as one of their own, no other wolf or beast whom he had always considered kindred are actually kin to him. The first lesson that Mowgli must learn is the lesson of betrayal by those whom he had considered friends. When at the wolf council there is an outcry against Mowgli continuing as a member of the pack, he has to lift high the 'red-flower', the fire that Bagheera had counselled him to get from the man-village, so that he may be safe from those he had considered brothers till then and from whose paws he had removed thorns from many times in the past.

Mowgli, reluctantly raising arms against those he considers kin, while filled with sorrow and rage within his heart, assumes the role of yet another Indian epic hero, *Arjuna*, who must shed kindred blood for the good of the world. Bagheera counselling an unsuspecting Mowgli of the dangers and treacherous ways of his 'wolf brothers' and asking him to secure his safety by getting fire is a veritable *Lord Krishna*, giving the warrior Arjuna the path of action in the face of all odds.

Kipling's Mowgli is a real and human character as he rages alone against the wolves at the wolf council and declares that: "I go from you to my own people—if they be my own people. The jungle is shut to me... But I will be more merciful than ye are... I promise that when I am a man among men I will not betray ye to men as ye have betrayed me... But remember when next I come to the Council Rock, as a man should come, it will be with Shere Khan's hide on my head."

Mowgli's dilemma is real and urgent in these lines as we realize that being disowned by the only home he had known all his life, Mowgli is left with no other, since it was only the first that he had ever known. Mowgli, banished to the man-village and adopted by the woman Messua as her lost son, must learn once again to become a man amongst men. He, who had always slept in the open on the ground or in tree branches as wild beasts do, suddenly finds himself confined inside a room on a soft bed that he finds uncomfortable.

Mowgli, born man, and brought up to be a wolf, finds himself neither. Moreover his familiarity with animals and his being spotted playing with his wolf brothers makes the villagers brand him a magician. Kipling here once again plays on the myth current in Indian villages where it was widely believed that magicians could turn themselves into wolves at will. It is this identity crisis that plays at the core of Mowgli's story.

Mowgli like the other famous Kipling character *Kim*, is a character on the crossroads of life. They both carry with them the burden of coming from two worlds and belonging to neither. In 'Mowgli's song' Kipling laments Mowgli's and perhaps his own dual-identity:

"As Mang flies between the Beasts and birds, so I fly between the village and the Jungle... These two things fight together in me as the snakes fight in the spring...I am two Mowglies".

There is to be no simple resolution to Mowgli's dilemma as shown in the Disney movie. After staying with the villagers and learning to be a man, Mowgli vanquishes his nemesis Shere Khan and returns triumphant to the Council Rock as he had promised. Mowgli assumes the role of the new leader of the pack and yet his inner conflicts are not all resolved.

Later, in *The Second Jungle Book*, in the story *Red Dog*, when the old wolf Akela remarks before dying that one day Mowgli on his own would return to be among men, a disturbed Mowgli cries: "Nay, nay, I am a wolf. I am of one skin with the Free people. It is no will of mine that I am a man".

We see how Mowgli would rather be a wolf, but is condemned to be a man. Akela's prophecy does come true, and Mowgli desires to be with his own kind as his heart is troubled with an unreasonable fear and sadness to see other beasts mating and frolicking with their own as nature calls to them in the garb of Spring, so that Mowgli runs alone through the forest to soothe this strange feeling, and ends up near the man village.

Though Kipling's Mowgli does find a human mate and settles down finally to a tame existence as a forest official under the aegis of the British government to a permanent salary and lifelong pension, he never really attains peace in his heart. Mowgli settles with his family on the fringes of the forest that had been both home and kingdom to him, and yet for him there is never really a sense of identification with either men or beasts.

One feels that Mowgli's complex sense of multiple identities, very much like Kipling's, results not so much in a sense of belonging but rather in an alienation that becomes an inextricable part of his identity.

For Kipling, the jungle in *The Jungle Books* was not merely a setting of adventure and imagination, but a microcosm of society itself. Kipling's jungle, unlike the Disney jungle, is not an Edenic Paradise but a brutal place where there is a constant struggle for existence. The jungle in Kipling's *The Jungle Books* stands as a complex, evocative metaphor whose full significance can hardly be grasped. Yet it is safe to assume that the jungle is a metaphor for a social set-up of society.

The Law of the Jungle which must be kept by one and all, high and low, is the social order that is necessary to stabilize and bind society, thus ensuring its smooth functioning. The critic Noel Annan has pointed out how Kipling in much of his work is preoccupied with 'what holds society together'. In *The Jungle Books*, it is clear that religion and custom, convention and morality, and laws are forces of social control. The individual breaks these rules at his own peril. The elephant Hathi, as old as the Jungle itself, Baloo, the wise teacher of the jungle laws, Akela, the leader of the wolf pack, Bagheera, the fearless and cunning warrior and also Kaa, the wily python, know the meaning and value of the jungle laws, and keep reminding Mowgli that he must respect them in order to survive the jungle.

In this sense, the jungle also becomes a metaphor for life itself. Kipling seems to imply that, as in the jungle, so also in life one can survive and succeed only if one understands, respects, and plays by the rules of the game. The narratorial voice of *The Jungle Books* constantly emphasises how *"The Law of the Jungle , which never orders anything without a reason"*, thus making it clear that The Law is the voice of sanity, of equilibrium, of peace and of stability there. The law is above all the creatures of the jungle and it is because of the Law that the jungle lives.

The canvas of *The Jungle Books,* as envisaged by Kipling, was way bigger for its adaptation in a two-hour movie. While apparently being written for children, the hidden narratives of the book were making it one of those controversial classics of its age which would continue to demand interpretations and explanations down the ages.

The Jungle Books carry with them Kipling's troubled legacy of an imperialist writer, but they nevertheless remain a deeply personal memoir of a writer who was bound to be reticent by nature. They are a legacy not only of a colonial past, but also of a wonderful childhood cut cruelly short by the vagaries of time. Embedded in the narrative of *The Jungle Books* is not only the imperialist ideology of the writer, but also the myths and folklores of a country which was a foster home to him.

Kipling's *The Jungle Books*, setting aside the rhetoric of Empire written in them, becomes the perfect example of the wonders which happen when cultures amalgamate. With Mowgli, Kipling was perhaps re-living the childhood that he never really had, a childhood which belonged to the distant warm place of his innocent past, a place he was to remember in his autobiography as a land "of daybreak, light and colour and golden and purple fruits at the level of my shoulder".

Chapter 2
The man behind The Jungle Books

As rich as the legacy and the history of *The Jungle Books* has been, there remains a yet greater tale to be told of the man who wrote them—Joseph Rudyard Kipling—the first British writer to be awarded the Nobel Prize for literature, in 1907.

Rudyard Kipling, the greatest till date of all Anglo-Indian writers, was born on 30 December 1865, in colonial India, in the bustling city of Bombay, which he was to describe in later years as:

"Mother of cities to me
For I was born at her gate,
Between the palms and the sea
Where the world-end steamers wait."

It was in one of these 'world-end steamers' that John Lockwood Kipling and Alice Kipling set sail for the British colony of India, on 10 April 1865, to seek their fortune. The Kiplings were sailing a long way from their home in England to the far East, perhaps with the same dreams that generations before them came with - of making a fortune in the fabled land of untold riches, unaware of the destiny that they were unconsciously bestowing on their eldest child.

*

The story of Kipling resonates across cultures, and even down the ages. For the story of his life is the story of the ordinary man who, with perseverance, his own talent and with a little luck, makes his fortune. The story of Kipling's life, right from his childhood to his youth and old age, is one of extraordinary courage in the face of life's challenges, which in his case began quite early. In his lifetime, Kipling remained a notoriously private man. He went out of his way to secure his personal history as his fame brought with it a slew of gold-diggers who saw money to be made on his name.

There are several biographies of Kipling, some authorised and some unauthorised, but here we attempt to understand the enigma of Kipling's personality based on what he himself had to say about it in his autobiography *Something for my*

Friends, Known and Unknown, which unfortunately remained unfinished with his sudden death.

Rudyard Kipling's encounter with India began even before his birth, because his mother was six weeks pregnant with him when his parents decided to cross the seas. Even Kipling's birth had that element of oriental mysticism which was to figure later in his writings, as he was finally ushered into the world after five days of painful labour, successful only when a sacrificial goat was offered at the shrine of the local Shiva temple by a family servant.

The boy was given the first name Joseph in accordance with the family tradition of giving the eldest male child of the family the name John/Joseph, while he was named Rudyard after the Rudyard reservoir in Staffordshire where his parents had first met. Rudyard was Ruddy to his parents and the close family circle, and grew up, like all Anglo-Indian kids, in the care of Indian servants – the Goan ayah who taught him to pray by the roadside cross and the Hindu bearer Meeta, who took him to the local Shiva temple.

The young Kipling was initiated early in the wonderful world of Indian folk-tales and myths by his Indian caretakers who, between them, pampered the young Sahib silly. Kipling was to remember the land of his birth as one of *"...daybreak, light and colour and golden and purple fruits at the level of my shoulder"*. It was this first impression of an early childhood that Kipling recorded in his autobiography.

This memory was, as Kipling explains, the memory of the Bombay fruit market where he went walking with his Indian nanny. It is interesting to note that these early impressions of childhood did not include his parents in any significant way. The parents, we see, come later in the shadows of these infant memories. Kipling remembered his mother as singing *"wonderful songs at a black piano"* and *'going out to Big Dinners"*, and his father as the kind man who consoled a younger Ruddy after the fright of an attack by a hen with a *'sketch and a rhyme'* about a little boy who was scared by a hen.

While Kipling refers to his ayah, his bearer, his sister and even his father as *'my ayah'*, *'Meeta, my Hindu bearer'*, *'my father'*, he refers to his mother with the respectful but distant *' the mother'*. This would perhaps point to the distance that he felt acutely as a child from his mother, who went about in the Anglo-Indian fashion of pursuing her own hobbies and interest and attending dinner parties while giving her child to the care of an Indian wet nurse and later an ayah. It would seem that it was only in the Goan ayah that Kipling had any real sense of a mother's presence.

He was to remember her yet again in his autobiography towards the end when he returned to his Bombay home as a well established writer, just before his marriage, to be welcomed again by "*my ayah, so old and so unaltered, met me with blessings and tears*". The father was to become in later years '*The Pater*', his sister was to him '*the child*' while his mother was to always remain '*the mother*'.

*

The circumstances of Kipling's birth in 1865 in colonial India, and his death in 1936 in London, where he lies buried in the poet's corner at Westminster Abbey, placed him not only on two geographical extremes, but also on a major epoch in the history of the world.

The span of Kipling's life, and the coincidences of his birth and death, saw him straddle the turn of the nineteenth century and the beginning of the twentieth. He came of an age as a writer when Britain was awakening to the wave of the 'new imperialism' — that phase of British imperial history from 1882 to 1906, during which the rise of other imperial rivals and the outbreak of nationalist uprisings throughout the Empire made the British government adopt a more self-conscious imperial policy.

This meant that the rampant plunder of the wealth of the colonised nations had to be tempered with the rhetoric of a 'benevolent' imperialism where the aim was to subdue and civilize the 'savage' races. Likewise in his middle age and at the height of his literary fame, Kipling was witness to the enormous strides that technology had started to take with the invention of new machines. Kipling was to touch on all of this and more in his literature, but the one abiding concern with which his name was to be forever associated was the project of the Empire itself.

Kipling was till the fag end of his life an apologist for the Empire. As Jorge Louis Borges wrote in 1941: *"Kipling's case is curious. For glory, but also as an insult, Kipling has been equated with the British Empire"*. In these lines, Borges was pointing out to the stupendous success that greeted Kipling as a writer of the Empire, as he churned out stories of India, and the later criticism that he had to face as the cult of the

Empire declined and its ideas became unpopular.

Kipling saw great success, and even greater criticism, in the course of his lifetime as public opinion changed course while he remained true to the force of his own convictions. It is unfortunate that his vast literary output, and even greater creative genius, remained circumscribed in the cult of the Empire which he professed. Kipling in his own lifetime was pronounced an imperialist and he never sought to explain his stance, but the narrowness of any such judgment on him is pointed out by him in his autobiography as he says:

> "Long ago I stated that 'East was East and West was West and never the twain should meet.' It seemed right for I had checked it by the card, but I was careful to point out circumstances under which cardinal points ceased to exist. Forty years rolled on, and for a fair half of them the excellent and uplifted of all lands would write me, apropos of each new piece of broad-minded folly in India, Egypt, or Ceylon, that East and West had met—as, in their muddled minds I suppose they had."

Kipling was not far from truth in saying that East

and West had not yet met and, even where they seemed to have met, it was but the superficial veneer of education and civilization, accessible but to the very few. It was yet to be some time, a long, long time before the seemingly parallel lines of the East and the West would meet on a greater footing of equality.

As much as Kipling was a writer of the Empire, he was more the creator of children's fiction. If it is only time which gives the true value of a writer then Kipling was a greater writer of children's literature than he was of the Empire. The popularity of the *Jungle Books*, *Kim*, *Just So Stories*, *Puck of Pooks Hill*, *Rewards and Fairies*, all children's stories, and read even today with the same pleasure as when they were written, would stand ample testimony to the truth of this statement. Yet readers would be surprised to know that this creator of such wonderful children literature was himself robbed of his childhood very early in life.

Life came to Kipling in fits and starts. Destiny somehow had a way of happening to Kipling when he least expected it. To put Kipling's life experiences in his own words:

"Looking back from this my seventieth year, it

seems to me that every card in my working life has been dealt to me in such a manner that I had to play it as it came."

In these pithy lines Kipling sums up the extraordinary highs and lows that life had dealt him.

Rudyard Kipling, born to John Lockwood Kipling and Alice Kipling, belonged to that bourgeois British middle class which came seeking a livelihood in India. Kipling was to bring alive the intricacies of the lives of this community of Anglo-Indians as they went about the business of Empire in a land that seemed hostile in the extremes of its hot weather. Through his special journalistic writing skills – a melange of fact and fiction – Kipling seemed to mirror in all its truth the British Empire of India, a colony which had somehow got associated with British pride and become a part of the Britain's national consciousness.

Kipling was to ride a sudden wave of fame which was to take him unawares. The early Indian short stories that Kipling wrote as a rookie journalist found a ready audience in India as well as in Britain, where there was a demand for his 'Indian stories', and led to what his sister Alice Macdonald Fleming was to describe years after his death as *"the Kipling Boom in 1890"*.

Kipling's keen observation of the hustle and bustle of life around him, combined with his journalistic skills, resulted in that brilliant portrayal of Anglo-India which was to remain unparalleled in the history of English literature. Kipling's realism and his unique 'insider' perspective seemed to mirror with true faith the Indian landscape. Kipling seemed to have opened the doors to the Indian subcontinent for a home grown British audience, whom he was to describe in his autobiography as a people who *"never looked further than their annual seaside resorts"*. But the mirror that Kipling held to India, though faithful, was at the same time contorted, since it mirrored this world as much through his myopic vision as the short sightedness of his larger political sensibilities.

Rudyard Kipling was India's prodigal son. It was India where he practised and learnt his trade. It was India which was his muse and his *daemon*. It was in his Indian stories that he was to live on years after his death. Kipling was to acknowledge this in his autobiography where he writes of India as *"the only real home I had yet known."* Later in life, when a very public spat with his American brother-in-law forced him to leave America to avoid the unwanted public scrutiny he was put under, he was to lament how: *"There are only two places in the world where I want to live – Bombay and Brattleboro. And I can't live in either"*.

Yet Kipling amply paid his debt to India by immortalising her in his books which, despite their evident prejudices, remain one of the most brilliant portrayals of colonial India. Kipling's India, bound as it is within the narrow confines of his prejudices, still overflows frequently with the rapturous outbursts of a soul which found solace in her.

With the sudden fame that overtook the Kipling family with their son's success in the literary world, there was also a natural curiosity about this precocious prodigy born in India who had stormed the literary scene. But Kipling was always wary of the ways of men and took to a systematic destruction of all his personal records and letters so as to uphold the sanity of the personal space where he gave vent to his creative urges. Kipling's obsessive destruction of all his personal records, and anxiety bordering on paranoia whenever there was an attempt to break into the vaults of his past, was looked down upon as unusual and misanthropic, but the world today should look rather with sympathy on him as a man who was trying to secure the sanctity of a life which had only recently found calm shores after being tossed on the waves of fortune.

Kipling significantly refers to the fame that he achieved as a writer as "*my notoriety*" in his autobiography. His general disapproval of the rummaging into his past was expressed by him:

> "When my notoriety fell upon me, there was a demand for my old proofs, signed and unsigned stuff not included in my books, and a general turning-out of refuse-bins for private publication and sale."

Just as reading had been the only joy to the six-year-old boy who found himself 'abandoned' by his parents among strangers in a cold land, so writing was a solace to the young man who, through the peculiarities of his own nature and the circumstances of his childhood, had grown up a recluse.

Writing was a release to Kipling, it was almost like meditation to him, and therefore too sacred to be treated lightly. Kipling recounts in his autobiography as to how in the second year of school at United Services College, Westward Ho!

"the tide of writing set in". It was also not for nothing that his English and Classics teacher named him in irritation "Gigadibs the literary man", a name that he was to proudly live up to.

Even as a young schoolboy at Westward Ho!, the myopic bespectacled Kipling, unfit for physical sports, could be seen "scribbling, so long as it had nothing to do with school work. He kept spoiling reams—absolute reams, not quires—of cream-laid notepaper for poems, because the lines were shortish and ended raggedly",

His school mate Beresford goes on to reminisce how, even then, Kipling was particular about maintaining the privacy of his writing as his "leather-bound books were guarded by a taboo".

In order to understand the dreams that fuelled the ambitions of young Kipling learning his trade in India, we need to go back once to what he refers to as a "*pivot*" experience which came with the realisation that he *"was a hireling paid to do what I was paid to do, and – I did not relish the idea"*. This turning point of his life Kipling described as the book *All in a Garden Fair* by Walter Besant.

Kipling goes on to say that this book came at a time of "*sore personal need"* when the depression of the Indian hot weather and the absence of a family away in the cool of Simla was getting on to him, as "*my salvation in sore personal need, and with the reading and re-reading it became to me a revelation, a hope and strength*". This book, in Kipling's own words, "*dealt with a young man who desired to write; who came to realise the possibilities of common things seen, and who eventually succeeded in his desire*".

In these lines, through a proxy literary hero, Kipling gives us the gist of his own literary ambitions as well as limitations.

For all his "notoriety", Kipling remained a simple man at heart and identified himself not with some great literary hero but with Robert Browning's poor orphan friar, Brother Fra Lippo-Lippi, who discovered he had the talent of drawing and to ease his head crammed full of pictures drew in astonishing detail all the faces that he had encountered in his lifetime.

Kipling speaks of Browning's literary creation saying, "*'Fra Lippo-Lippi', a not too remote—I dare to think – ancestor of mine*". In the bleak six years of life at his foster home in Southsea, books came as solace and writing as a release of pent-up emotions. In Kipling's own words:

"Nor was my life an unsuitable preparation for my future, in that it demanded constant wariness, the habit of observation, and attendance on moods and tempers; the noting of discrepancy between speech and action; a certain reserve of demeanour; an automatic suspicion of sudden automatic favours. Brother Lippo Lippi, in his own harder case, as a boy discovered—

Why, soul and sense of him grow sharp alike
He learns the look of things, and none the less
For admonition."

Brother Lippo-Lippi's case was hard since he was an orphan starving in the streets, but the young Kipling's case was harder still, for he was the greater 'orphan' of the two: he had known loving parents who, though far away, still wrote letters to him and his sister telling that they were much loved and missed, and yet parents who had condemned them to a cruel exile from which *"there seemed to be no getting out"* without any warning or explanation.

Kipling's identification with Browning's character is more revealing of Kipling the man than a hundred biographies could ever faithfully profess to tell. Kipling's reference to Browning's poems is an indirect allusion to the story of his early childhood, and also the pointer to a trail that leads one right onto the wells of creativity from which Kipling the writer drew. The one enduring note of Kipling's life had been the sense of losing those who were closest to his heart. His first loss was as a six-year-old, who lost the kingdom of his parents Edenic Indian home and the fiefdom of his beloved ayah and Hindu bearer who were a ready stock of wonderful Indian tales.

According to the fashion of the times, the six-year-old Kipling and his even younger sister were sent 'home' to England in the care of a foster family so that the children could have a British education and upbringing and so grow up to be 'properly' British. To the young Kipling, this loss was to shape and define his life and thoughts for all the years of his life. Kipling was to describe this foster home in his autobiography as the "*House of Desolation*".

Kipling lived there for nearly six years, his only solace being the memory of his Indian years and that of his ayah and the bearer Meeta with their "*stories and Indian nursery songs all unforgotten*". Such was the impact of these six years that, writing his autobiography in his seventieth year, he was to remember those years like this:

"I had never heard of Hell, so I was introduced to it in all its terrors... I have known a certain amount of bullying, but this was calculated torture."

Trix, Kipling's young sibling and fellow sufferer was to recall the horrors of life at the foster home in Southsea a few months after her brother's death, in the short story *Through Judy's Eyes*, a companion piece to Kipling's own account of those harrowing days in the intensely autobiographical short story *Baa Baa Black Sheep*. Trix, or rather Alice Macdonald Fleming, as was her married name, was to reveal in a candid radio broadcast talk on the BBC entitled, *My Brother Rudyard Kipling*, how this 'abandonment' by their parents was to be forever the pivot around which everything else that followed in her and her brother's life was to revolve. In Mrs Fleming's own words:

"It is eleven years since my brother Rudyard Kipling died, and as the slow years lengthen I find I no longer dwell on the Kipling Boom in 1890... I take refuge rather in our very early days together when a sturdy little boy, not quite six and a spoilt baby of three and a half—that

was me—were left by their parents, who were
going back to India, to face a cold world,
without one familiar face. And we were left with
strangers who were very unkind to us."

Alice Macdonald Fleming (Kipling) has been
quoted extensively here because, in her voice, we
can hear what her illustrious brother always left
unsaid. Alice Kipling was related to her brother
not only by ties of blood, but by the greater bond
that ties co-sufferers, especially when they are as
painfully young as the Kipling siblings were. She
goes on to relate how *"The real tragedy... sprang
from our inability to understand why our parents
had deserted us... it was like a double death, or
rather like an avalanche that had swept away
everything happy and familiar... There was no
getting out of that, as we often said."*

The Southsea years were difficult for both
young Rudyard and Trix Kipling, but perhaps
more so for the precocious boy who was singled
out for punishments not only by the lady of the
house, but also her son, the troubles of which were
compounded by a rapidly failing eyesight. Yet
Kipling was never to speak directly of this past,
and indeed of anything concerned with his
personal life. It is with regard to this that Alice

Kipling's account, and moreover its timing, is so significant.

Though the Kipling siblings were rescued from that dungeon of childhood nightmare, it seemed that in reality there never was any real *"getting out of that"* for them. Rudyard Kipling never in his lifetime let the mask of stoic indifference to the world's opinion drop. The hurt of those years, and the intensity of the damage it wrought on young minds, was revealed only once at the age of twenty three, when the suppressed emotional hurt of those years exploded in the intimately biographical story, *Baa Baa Black Sheep*. The writing of this story must have come as a cathartic release of all those pent up emotions which were threatening to annihilate all that was good and beautiful in his life.

In *Baa Baa Black Sheep*, Rudyard took the character of Punch, while his little sister and fellow sufferer was characterised as *Judy*. The story which begins on a desperately bleak note ends in hope with the return of the absent mother. But even as Punch reassures his sister that, "we *are as much Mother's as if she had never gone"*, a background voice ominously declares: *"Not altogether, O Punch, for when young lips have drunk deep of the waters of Hate, Suspicion and*

Despair, all the Love in this world, will not wholly take away that knowledge".

Here perhaps all of Kipling's readers would understand the foreboding sense of menace and the struggle for existence that clouds even the most happy of his children's stories, certainly in *The Jungle Books* and *Kim* . Perhaps it is these childhood experiences that gave birth to *Mowgli* and *Kim*—abandoned but fearless children who carved out their destinies on their own, much like their creator Rudyard Kipling did himself.

*

His second loss was less evident, but no less than the first one—that of his beloved sister, his only connection to that beautiful Indian past, who in spite of being under the same roof was worlds apart, shelled in the cocoon of her own fears, seeking refuge in obedience to the cruel foster mother who warned her against talking with her brother.

Other, more personal and heart-rending losses came later in life with the death of his beloved first born at the tender age of six, his daughter Josephine, *"the delight of his heart"*, to whose memory he was to dedicate *The Jungle Books*. The mental breakdown of his beloved sister Trix, the death of his parents and later the death of his only son and third child John, who was declared missing in the First World War, were other defining moments of his life.

Kipling's close relation with books and the ambivalence of his attitude towards the world of men is made plain enough in his autobiography. He identifies himself with literary heroes, and while relating anecdotes from his public life he speaks as a spectator rather than as a participant. To quote Kipling himself:

> "It seemed best to stand clear of it all. For that reason, I have never directly or indirectly criticised any fellow-craftsman's output, or encouraged any man or woman to do so; nor have I approached any persons that might be led to comment on my output. My acquaintance with my contemporaries has from the first to last been very limited."

The privacy that Kipling wanted in life was perhaps a consequence of the bitterness of the experiences that he had with the world outside his own inner family circle. The extreme reluctance to share with the public any details of his personal life drew perhaps from the fear of unwanted censor that he had faced nearly all his life. Apart from the painful memories of childhood, even his school life was not as smooth, for he somehow stood apart from his fellow schoolmates in his spectacles, uncommon then, which gave him the nickname *'Gigger'* after gig lamps which his bottle-lensed spectacles resembled.

Even later in life. working for the *Civil and Military Gazette* in Lahore, India, as the only representative of his paper at the Punjab Club round which his social life revolved, he often found himself the object of ridicule for the government policies, contrary to popular public opinion, that his state-owned paper endorsed. Kipling recounts this in his autobiography and says: "*It is not pleasant to sit still when one is twenty while all your universe hisses you*".

Even as a well established writer, he was charged with being a little too money minded, which is why he makes it a point to clarify that the set of verses titled *Recessional* were *'given'* by him to *The Times* without any charges and goes on to say:

"It does not much matter what people think of a man after his death, but I should not like the people whose good opinion I valued to believe that I took money for verses on Joseph Chamberlain, Rhodes, Lord Milner, or any of my South African verse in *The Times.*"

Another abiding concern of Kipling's life was India itself, the country he was born in, the land that nurtured him, and the landscape and the people who were gave fire to his imagination. Kipling's was a never-ending affair with India—the land that was both mother and mistress to him. India was a mother for it was in her lap that he was born in the bustling metropolis of Bombay, growing up as a 'native' sahib, speaking the vernacular by choice and English by compulsion.

India became a mistress to him when the young sahib, who had left her shores at about six years of age, returned a whiskered young man of "*sixteen years and nine months, but looking four or five years older, and adorned with real whiskers*", to apprentice with his "*first mistress and most true love, the little Civil and Military Gazette*" at Lahore.

It was in those days of apprenticeship that he lost himself in the dark alleys and byways of the city, beckoned by the seductive secret life of the night. And like everything and everyone that was dearest to him, he never ever spoke openly of or about India.

Kipling's love-hate relationship with the country was to end in a life-long love affair—affirmed by him in his unfinished autobiography—*Something of Myself, For my Friends Known and Unknown*. As one courses through the pages of this work, the well-calculated words and sentences reluctantly describing a life obscure which suddenly came into the spotlight of fame and success, one encounters a longing for the lost Indian 'home' which surfaces in strange ways wherever the authors life takes him.

Kipling hints at his close attachment to India in the very first line of the autobiography which goes: "*Give me the first six years of a child's life and you can have the rest*", the reference being obviously to his early Indian years. The narrative begins with an invocation to the Muslim God with: "*Therefore, ascribing all good fortune to Allah the Dispenser of Events, I begin*".

Herein it is made obvious that Kipling identified himself more as an Indian Muslim rather than as the Christian that he was born. He recalls an anecdote from his South African sojourn during the Boer War when, on a train journey, he encountered the Muslim servant of an Indian officer whose conscience was troubled on the point of eating the tinned beef that he was given to eat and whose conscience he eased by telling him: *"when Islam wars with unbelievers, the Koran permits reasonable latitude of ceremonial obligations; and he did not hesitate,"* showing the thoroughness of his knowledge of the Indian Muslim.

Readers familiar to his work would definitely recognise the Muslim's disgust of the 'wily' Hindu that runs as a recurrent theme in his characterisation of Hindus, especially the priestly class. This is significant considering the ambivalences that lay at the core of Kipling's own personality. Kipling explains this:

> "But the North-west provinces, as they were then, being largely Hindu, were strange 'air and water' to me. My life had lain among Muslims, and a man leans one way or other according to his first service".

Unfortunately, Kipling's undeniable literary genius was often marred by this sort of prejudiced 'leanings' regarding races and nations that often appears in his works.

*

Fascination with India is clear throughout his autobiography. Even when the narrative moves from India to Southsea, India lingers in the in the memories of the disconsolate child as a lost land of wonder and excitement. The narrative gains pace and excitement only when it returns once again to India in the author's sixteenth year and remains there for a complete seven years, the years of Kipling's apprenticeship as a writer. Then it returns once again to London as the writer seeks his fortune there, just as his parents had come decades ago from that country seeking their fortune in India.

Even then, India reappears sometimes in the night song of the guard and sometimes in the workings of the state machinery which curiously remind Kipling of his experiences in India, and sometimes even in a bout of severe influenza when *"all my Indian microbes joined hands and sang for a month in the darkness of Villiers Street"*.

Later in life, when Kipling sought refuse from the cold of England in the South African city of Cape Town, the description of the land as *"the dry, spiced smell of the land and the smack of the clean sunshine were health restoring"*, sounds familiarly like India. Likewise in Australia, the occasional burst of hot wind is compared to "*the loo of the Punjab*".

Kipling's canvas and his tools of art were the men that he daily observed. He had indeed practiced life as he preached it in his inspirational poem "*If...*". He had indeed talked with crowds and kept his virtue and walked with kings without losing the common touch. But, however great his literary talents were, they had their own limitations too. He was a trader of words and had wares for every occasion, but he was definitely not up to the demands of the time. His own limited vision, and even limited social circle, combined with a reluctance to look outside the comfort zone of his own ideas, marred his literary genius.

It was his prejudiced, narrow outlook which branded him an 'imperialist'. He was at his best a magnifying mirror to the world as he saw it, and he excelled in bringing the humdrum existence of life to a realistic portrayal in his books, with a touch of the writer's creativity. Yet we should still remember him as a faithful chronicler of the imperial experience, and moreover the genius of many wonderful stories which have filled our leisure with the joy of reading them.

Chapter 3
Who is Mowgli?

"*The Only Son lay down again and dreamed that he dreamed a dream...*

'Now, was I born of womankind and laid in a mother's breast?

For I have dreamed of a shaggy hide whereon I went to rest.

And was I born of womankind and laid on a father's arm?

For I have dreamed of long white teeth that guarded me from harm.

Oh, was I born of womankind and did I play alone?

For I have dreamed of playmates twain that bit me to the bone....

'Tis a League and a league to the Lena Falls where the trooping sambhur go,

But I can hear the little fawn that bleats behind the doe!

'Tis a league and a league to the Lena Falls where the crop and the upland meet,

But I can smell the warm wet wind that

whispers through the wheat!' "
Rudyard Kipling, 'The Only Son'

These lines from Kipling's *In the Rukh* sings of the inner conflict of a grown up Mowgli, who – though outwardly leading the normal life of a householder – still struggles in his heart with the question: 'Who is Mowgli'?

The man-cub of *The Jungle Books* is now a man with children of his own and yet the one enduring question of Mowgli's life remains unresolved. The song which has a dream like quality is actually the interpretation of a nightmare that awakens a sleeping Mowgli. It points to the one eternal truth of Mowgli's life—that he belongs to two worlds.

The similarity here between Mowgli's situation and the circumstances of Kipling's own life is hard to miss. While the song quietly questions the origins of Mowgli, his birth in the man-village and upbringing by the wolves in the jungle in the first half, there is a clear note of heartfelt yearning for a lost land of childhood that is evident in the second half of the poem.

Mowgli's memory of the 'shaggy hide' of the mother wolf *Raksha*, on which he rested instead of the warm breast of the mother who gave birth to him, and his memory of the white fangs of the father wolf who kept all harm away from him, instead of the protective strong arms of the biological father that children normally know, would remind readers of Kipling's own short childhood in India in the care of native servants.

Mowgli, much like Kipling, had known first the ways and tongue of his foster family. Whereas for Mowgli it was the jungle, for Kipling it was India, the land of his birth. It is an interesting coincidence to note that, just as Bagheera bought Mowgli's life and safety in the wolf-pack with the flesh of a young bull, so Kipling's birth, after a long failed labour, was successful only with the sacrifice of a goat at the local deity's shrine.

Mowgli is naturalised to the ways of the jungle and learns the ways of men much later in life when he is ousted from there at the wolf-council by the new wolves for being a 'man'. Kipling too was exiled to cold, dark London from his Edenic Indian home, so that he might learn the manners and ways of the British and grow up to be a 'white' man. Even later in *The Jungle Book*, we see how Mowgli returns to the jungle to rule it only to leave it again on a self imposed exile, just as Kipling had returned to India and then left it forever to settle in London.

The similarities between Mowgli and Kipling

here seem to be more than mere coincidence. Kipling may have been putting more of himself in the man-cub Mowgli than he himself realised. Because, for Kipling, the writing of the Mowgli stories in *The Jungle Books* was a mystical experience. He was to write in his autobiography how the Mowgli stories just grew out of his pen, as if there were was a jinn released through his writing the stories of the wolf-boy Mowgli.

Kipling firmly believed that the Mowgli stories were the work of the 'daemon' who resided within him. With characteristic humour and humility, Kipling says in his autobiography how very often in life he had wondered at much that was published with his name and if it was really he who had the brilliance to write all that.

The writing of *The Jungle Books*, dedicated by Kipling to his dead eldest child, the daughter Josephine, must have been a very personal experience for the writer. Just as reading books had once rescued him from the dungeons of despair in the bleak years of childhood in Southsea, so writing books also came as a release to the writer in the later years of his youth and old age. Writing was for Kipling a catharsis of sorts, as he gave to the written word the closest secrets of his heart. For a man, whose circumstances in life made him suspicious of the ways of men, writing came naturally as an outlet for emotions that were seldom shared.

The corpus of Kipling's work is huge. Although a phenomenal literary success story in his own times, Kipling was lost to the world in the years that saw the decline of the cult of empire. Kipling was a staunch believer in the idea of 'benevolent' imperialism, something that he was to phrase infamously as 'the white-man's burden'. With the fall of the empire, when ideas of imperialism became unpopular, Kipling was relegated to the shadows of oblivion.

Although dismissed by his contemporaries like George Orwell, who famously called him a *'flag waver'* and a *'jingoistic imperialist'*, the embers of Kipling's dying fame were kept alive by his last two Indian works—*The Jungle Books* and *Kim*.

In Kipling's characterisation of the Irish hero Kim, *'little friend of all the world'* in the novel of the same name, was read for long and widely as a presentation of the Indian years of Kipling's childhood. But Kipling had hidden a truer self in the character of Mowgli and placed him in the dark jungle of *The Jungle Books* where he thrived uncensored for long by the prying eyes of critics.

If Kipling gave to Kim the *joie de vivre* of his

early childhood in India, he gave to Mowgli the pain of the lost years of innocence in Southsea, and the scepticism and struggles of life as a young adult out to prove his worth to the world. It was the semi-autobiographical and purely human core of both these stories that kept them alive, even when the tide of Kipling's fame had ebbed.

The two enduring notes of Kipling's life were the Empire and India. While it was to the cause of the first that he dedicated his life, it was to the second that he owed it. There is an apparent incongruity between these two facts, but for Kipling they were the parallel ways to a similar end. It is necessary to understand here that for Kipling the 'Empire' was not a commercial enterprise, but a human endeavour aimed at bettering our world.

The Empire was to him a central authority, a stabilizing force, a bridge between nations, a necessary consequence of the white man's superiority over other races of the world. Although his ideas would seem outrageous to a modern reader, they were the natural corollary to a discourse in the western world which took roots with Darwin's theory of the *Origin of the Species* and the survival of the fittest in the natural world.

Kipling's birth, and moreover his work in and

on India, resulted in his being considered an unofficial authority on colonial India and its people. The presentation speech in honour of Kipling's being conferred with the Nobel Prize for literature in 1907 for his novel *Kim*, said how he had captured in his works: *"the strenuous pulsating life of our times, that life which is often chequered and fretted by the painful struggle for existence and all its concomitant worries and embarrassments"*.

The citation went on to declare:

"The firm grasp of the true inwardness of all things Indian is abundantly reflected in Kipling's writings, so much so that it has even been said that they have brought India nearer home to the English nation, than has the construction of the Suez Canal."

The Nobel citation for Kipling has been quoted here both as a reminder of the power of ideas as they spread through the written word, as also to the politics of representation. The literary corpus of Kipling's writing is formidable, both in its bulk and in its authenticity. The catch is that, even as the 'insider', Kipling was looking only on the outer show of things. He never did in reality penetrate the inner life of the world that he was putting a mirror up to.

He knew and spoke best of the Anglo-Indian life, the workings of the government machinery and of soldiers, all of which he came to see from close quarters as a journalist. As regards the native populace, he had access only to the extremes— either in his personal capacity as a master to his servant, or as a journalist to the sundry Indian princes scattered throughout India who lived in collusion with the British rulers.

His travels no doubt brought him into close contact with the newly emerging educated Indian bourgeoisie which was coming mostly from Bengal, but he scorned them in the fashion of the true-blue British that he presented himself as. One of these has been famously caricatured by him as *Hurree Babu* in the novel *Kim*.

The bourgeoisie, which as the history of the world has proved time and again, is the driving force behind the awakening of the nations of our world, is sadly, and rather consciously, missing in Kipling's work. Kipling's *Kim*, while indeed portraying the 'strenuous pulsating life' of the times was also playing along to several stereotypes about the East prevalent in the Western world. The innocence of Kim, much like most of Kipling's literary works, is marred by the obvious agenda of empire that had a way of creeping in all that he wrote.

*

The circumstances of Kipling's life and work made him heir to two worlds—that of colonised India and of colonising Britain. His vast literary output took its inspiration from the sights and sounds of colonial India. Kipling's journalistic story-telling, combined with his penchant for realism give his stories the veneer of authenticity, which imparted to his writing a certain power and influence. Kipling was, as we all are, a product of his own particular age.

But, unlike ordinary men, the literary man becomes the voice and the face of the times he writes in. Kipling remained a strong votary of empire until the end of his life, apparently oblivious to a rapidly changing world.

It may have been his own way of clinging on to the one ideal of his youth while his personal life was torn apart with the string of losses that began with the death of his daughter and ended with the death of an only son in the Great War. After a lifetime trying to conform to certain prescribed ideals, this obstinate advocacy of the empire was perhaps an act of defiance in not conforming to the new ideas that were sweeping across the world.

It might seem ironic that a man, who was read as an imperialist even after his death, was to create a piece of work which was to be interpreted as a classic multicultural movie experience. The Mowgli stories in *The Jungle Books*, adapted and presented by Walt Disney, stands today as one of the cultural artefacts of our age.

It is exactly because of this that it needs a re-visioning and re-interpretation every once in a while as the paradigms of human knowledge change. It is Kipling's own diversity of upbringing and the ambiguities of his personal life and literary output that result from it which makes him relevant to our times.

Kipling's wrote as the first true citizen of the world, 'the only son', who belonged both to the East and the West. In his literary heroes, especially Mowgli, we see first explored the complexities of belonging to two worlds at the same time.

*

In his autobiography, Kipling speaks of one of his works for children called *Rewards and Fairies*, a historical fantasy in the children's fiction genre:

> "Since the tales had to be read by children, before people realised that they were meant for grownups; and since they have to be a sort of balance to as well as a seal upon, some aspects of my 'Imperialistic' output in the past, I worked the material in three or four overlaid tints and textures, which might or might not reveal themselves according to the shifting light of sex, youth, and experience."

One can safely assume that these very lines apply even to *The Jungle Books*.

Kipling's *The Jungle Books* have been read as allegories of empire and rightly so, for there is an unmistakeable hierarchy in the presentation of the animals. The 'Jungle Law' that rules the community of wolves and other animals of the jungle, excepting the outcast monkey-folk, is understood to be a sort of allegorical presentation of the British rule in India.

The monkeys who disrupt the peace of the jungle with their nefarious plans have been interpreted as the rebel native Indians. It is obvious that the empire allegory looks back to the Indian Mutiny of 1857. It is part of the problematic legacy that Kipling has left behind him that, while reading his works, one is drawn suspiciously to find motives of the Empire.

So when we read the Mowgli stories as an allegory of the Empire, we often overlook the human tale that lies at the core of the stories—the tale of an orphan boy who is reared among strangers (wolves). Mowgli is raised by wolves and he grows up believing he is one, only to find himself ousted from the wolf-pack for being a man.

And when he goes to the man-village, his peculiarities set him apart from other men who pronounce him a sorcerer so that he is driven out of the village too by the 'man-pack'.

Mowgli's journey through *The Jungle Books* is a quest for the answer to the question: "Who is Mowgli"? He is, as he says, a brother to the wolves "all but in blood", but then there are strange yearnings in his heart which forbid him killing man, as the Law of the Jungle forbids killing one's own kind, and yet he hates men and their ways with a vengeance.

There are many underlying shades to Kipling's Mowgli, a character in which he put more of himself than he has in his other Irish-Indian hero Kim, who has been more frequently compared to the reticent writer. Long years after the decline of the Empire, Mowgli and Kim thrive because of this human element in them that appeal universally beyond the artificial barriers of race and culture.

Mowgli's search for his identity remains the central theme in the Mowgli stories in *The Jungle Books*. As Mowgli navigates the crisis of his identity which seemed to change overnight for him from being that of a wolf to a man, Kipling was not only interrogating the demons of his personal life, but also putting forward one of the enduring concerns of the modern world. Mowgli was born in the golden dawn of the era of globalisation, when the progress of science and technology had started opening up the boundaries of the world.

In the present scenario, as technology brings the communities of the world into instant contact with the click of a mouse, our world truly becomes a global village. But the flipside of this technology boom is the way in which the diversity of our world is often in an open confrontation which makes our world more of a global jungle, than a global village, where the ruthless law of nature gives sustenance only to those ideas that it deems the fittest.

*

The story *Letting in the Jungle*, in *The Second Jungle Book,* which includes Mowgli's revenge for the way in which the village has ousted him and his adoptive family, holds a grave lesson for our world even today. The wrath that Mowgli unleashes on the man-village after his successful return to the jungle is a reminder to the ways in which man's mind may work when it is despised and racially segregated.

We live in a world that has witnessed the rapacious plunder of colonialism, dictators, and two devastating world wars while standing even today on the nervous edge of a precipice where a nuclear war can be declared any moment. This results naturally in a wry scepticism and a fear of the 'other'.

The closer we come together as a people, the greater is the urgency of seeking the shelter of familiar beliefs and faiths. It is as Manuel Castells says in *'The Information Age*: "Our world and our lives are being shaped by the conflicting trends of globalisation and identity."

The exposure to a connected world that technology provides makes us belong severally to various cultures, creeds and beliefs which do not subscribe naturally to the ideas with which we have been brought up. While 'the information age' makes us more aware of our surroundings and broad in our mental outlook, it is this very exposure, and the public censure of certain religious or personal beliefs, that gives rise to the fundamentalist instincts which threaten to tear apart the social fabric of our world.

In these turbulent times, we need to turn towards the man-cub Mowgli whose journey between the jungle and the man-village ominously foretells of our own world. Mowgli's quest for his identity resonates with our own selves as we try to negotiate the contingencies of our own existence and helps us become truly deserving citizens of our world.

The question of identity has become more urgent now than it was ever before. Identity is both social and personal. It takes roots in our private lives that we begin as an individual in a family, and it flowers and spreads its branches in our social interactions as with age we grow out of, and into, ideas that we assimilate from our environment. As John Tomlinson points out in his essay, *Globalisation and Cultural Identity:*

"Identity is not in fact merely some fragile

communal-psychic attachment, but a considerable dimension of **institutionalised** social life in modernity".

Tomlinson is here pointing out how identity formation which starts with the family is our induction into the primary unit of the larger organisation of society and the state. But, as Mowgli's story would teach us, the family – by which is meant those who nurture and protect the fragile and easily impressed infancy of our childhood – gives the foundations to our identity.

The Mowgli stories are an epic narrative of successful survival against all the odds. As a child who belongs to two opposing worlds, Mowgli presents the challenges of integration in a society that limits itself to its own rigid boundaries. Mowgli is the face of two opposing worlds which in a curious twist of fate find themselves assimilated in his person.

Mowgli at once belongs to both these worlds without belonging completely to either. It is in this conflict of his soul, that tugs once this way and then towards the other way, that Mowgli becomes one amongst us, the dual-faced inhabitants of a world where transient notions of supposed superiority or inferiority guide our choices. In the existential identity crisis of life that Mowgli finds himself in, not knowing who he is or where he belongs, the Law of the Jungle comes as a guiding light. The Law of the Jungle holds eternally true and is universal in its application. The Law recognizes the diversity and multiplicity of the world and is the guarantee of peace and harmony between all creatures.

The Law of the Jungle as taught to Mowgli by the wise bear Baloo is one of the most valuable lessons that one takes away from *The Jungle Books*. It is in an understanding of the Jungle Law that the essence of Kipling's creed lies, a creed that knows only the cult of humanity and preaches peaceful co-existence. Any attempts at interpreting the Law, as given by Kipling, takes away from its beauty and therefore it is quoted here as it is. This is how *The Law of the Jungle* goes:

"Now this is the Law of the Jungle – as old and as true as the sky;

And the Wolf that shall keep it may prosper, but the Wolf that shall break it must die.

As the creeper that girdles the tree-trunk the Law runneth forward and back -

For the strength of the Pack is the Wolf, and

the strength of the Wolf is the Pack.

Wash daily from nose-tip to tail-tip; drink deeply, but never too deep;

And remember the night is for hunting, and forget not the day is for sleep.

The jackal may follow the Tiger, but, Cub, when thy whiskers are grown,

Remember the Wolf is a hunter – go forth and get food of thine own.

Keep peace with the Lords of the Jungle – the Tiger, the Panther, the Bear;

And trouble not Hathi the Silent, and mock not the Boar in his Lair.

When Pack meets with Pack in the Jungle, and neither will go from the trail,

Lie down till the leaders have spoken – it may be fair words shall prevail.

When ye fight with a Wolf of the Pack, ye must fight him alone and afar,

Lest others take part in the quarrel, and the Pack be diminished by war.

The Lair of the Wolf is his refuge, and where he has made him his home,

Not even the Head Wolf may enter, not even the Council may come.

The Lair of the Wolf is his refuge, but where he has digged it too plain,

The Council shall send him a message, and so he shall change it again.

If ye kill before midnight, be silent, and wake not the woods with your bay,

Lest ye frighten the deer from the crops, and the brothers go empty away.

Ye may kill for yourselves, and your mates, and your cubs as they need, and ye can;

But kill not for pleasure of killing, and SEVEN TIMES NEVER KILL MAN.

If ye plunder his Kill from a weaker, devour not all in thy pride;

Pack-Right is the right of the meanest; so leave him the head and the hide.

The Kill of the Pack is the meat of the Pack. Ye must eat where it lies;

And no one may carry away of that meat to his lair, or he dies.

The Kill of the Wolf is the meat of the Wolf. He may do what he will,

But, till he has given permission, the Pack may not eat of that Kill.

Cub-Right is the right of the Yearling. From all of his Pack he may claim

Full-gorge when the killer has eaten; and none may refuse him the same.

Lair-Right is the right of the Mother. From all

of her year she may claim

One haunch of each kill for her litter, and none may deny her the same.

Cave-Right is the right of the Father – to hunt by himself for his own.

He is freed of all calls to the Pack; he is judged by the Council alone.

Because of his age and his cunning, because of his gripe and his paw,

In all that the Law leaveth open, the word of the Head Wolf is Law.

Now these are the Laws of the Jungle, and many and mighty are they;

But the head and the hoof of the Law and the haunch and the hump is – Obey!"

When we read the Law of the Jungle, we realise how the Mowgli stories were not merely an allegory of the empire for Kipling, but more the allegory of life itself. The Law repeated in a sing-song voice might lull the infant Mowgli to sleep, but heard again and again and internalised in his being, it becomes a guardian philosophy for life. Kipling did not look at life with rose-tinted glasses, but with the clear hard stare of the experiences that life gave him. The Law of the Jungle which every beast must follow are the rules that bind society together. They carry in their edicts the maxims of non-violence, brotherhood and goodwill to all.

Each creature of the jungle is bound to the other in the cycle of life where one must prey on the other for food, but apart from the contingencies of this rule of Nature, the Law is a humane code of conduct, a way of living a dignified life, and it provides for each creature according to its worth.

The significance of the Law is underlined once again in the last lesson that Mowgli's old teacher Baloo gives him, as Mowgli leaves the jungle for the man-village, a lesson that would hold him in good stead as the jungle bids him farewell for the new hunting that he must do in the man-village. Baloo's song, heard as a distant voice in the jungle, as Mowgli makes his way to the man-village goes like this:

*"For the sake of him who showed
One Wise Frog the Jungle-Road
Keep the Law the Man-Pack make—
For thy blind old Baloo's sake!*
...
*When thy Pack would make thee pain,
Say:'Tabaqui sings again'.*

When thy Pack would work thee ill,
Say 'Shere Khan is yet to kill'.
When the knife is drawn to slay,
Keep the Law and go thy way."

In this last edict of the Law that Baloo gives to Mowgli, he not only foresees the challenges that Mowgli will face in adapting to a new 'pack', but also shows him the way out, which lies not in confrontation but in patient conciliation. In the wise words of Baloo, Kipling speaks himself because he understood the need to respect the culture of the 'other'.

The 'Law' of the jungle in this instance becomes synonymous with the cultural diversity of the world which must be respected in all circumstances. The jungle *Law*, it would seem, holds some very important lessons for our world where increased exposure to the 'Law' of the other results in conflicts.

*

From the Jungle Laws, it is but a natural progression to the 'Master of the Jungle' himself, Mowgli. As we have seen, Kipling put more of himself in Mowgli than has been credited. The existential crisis of Kipling's own dual identity finds a more true reflection in the man-cub Mowgli, than in the other Kipling hero Kim, in whose characterisation the reclusive author has been much sought.

Mowgli is a character that grows during the course of the tales. In the characterisation of his dilemmas and the duality of his being that Mowgli faces, Kipling was perhaps giving to the world of literature its first postmodern hero. Mowgli's search for his true self as he negotiates the duality of his identity, feeling himself a 'wolf' trapped in the body of man, reflects the existential crisis of man's existence that literature was to explore later.

Although the wise leader of the wolf pack Akela, knows that Mowgli must one day return to his own kind, Mowgli himself refuses to believe in Akela's prophetic words, and chooses to live in the jungle as the leader of the wolf pack, and indeed of all the jungle creatures, even the old elephant Hathi, after he defeats Shere Khan and rids the jungle of the menace of the Red Dhole dogs of the Deccan.

Mowgli lives as a wolf among wolves, the undeclared king of the jungle. The critical moment in *Spring Running*, when Mowgli feels a strange emptiness within and decides that he must go to the man-village, it is the unmistakeable call of spring that beckons him.

Mowgli leaves the jungle, though he loves it, because the jungle can give him all that he desires but not the mate who would complete him. Mowgli leaves the jungle to find his mate, and then returns to familiarize his 'home' to the mate he has chosen. Mowgli never really leaves the jungle, although he seems to do so, for the jungle lives in his soul. We see how he builds a home for himself and his family on the fringes of the jungle. The forest is forever open to embrace him as and when he chooses to do so.

He never really becomes 'man' in the proper sense of the word, though he does put on the outward show of being one.

The 'jungle' and the 'man-village' in the Mowgli stories are also two contesting cultural spaces. Mowgli has the unique privilege of having an access to both these worlds. For Mowgli, to change from a 'wolf' to a 'man' means negotiating the social and cultural barriers that divides these different spaces. Both these social spaces come with their particular code of conduct and acceptable behaviour to which its inhabitants must adhere.

Thus Mowgli, who is used to sleeping in the

open on the hard ground, must learn that men sleep on soft beds in enclosed shelters. The wise teacher of the jungle Law, Baloo, in his last lesson to Mowgli when he leaves the jungle, tells him that he must follow the rules of the man-pack in the village, just as he had that of the wolf-pack in the jungle.

Although inhabiting a common universe, the jungle and the man-village are two different worlds. It would seem that they are the 'East' and the 'West' of Kipling's imagination and 'never the twain shall meet'.

But Kipling had envisioned a different ending to Mowgli's story. It is not in Mowgli that the East and the West of the jungle and the village meet, but there is a ray of hope in Mowgli's children who can be often seen playing with the mighty grey wolves who come visiting them. Kipling seems to imply a near future, somewhere on the horizon, where these two opposing worlds reconcile.

Mowgli's children inherit from their mother the customs of the man-village and learn from their father 'the Law of the Jungle' and the various tongues in which the jungle speaks. Although not overtly expressed, Kipling implies as much in the scene of domestic felicity with which he draws the curtains on Mowgli's story.

And though Kipling did not live long enough to see this wonderful meeting of the East and the West, he would no doubt have had a new magical tale in his pen about the lives of Mowgli's children had he lived.

Bibliography

Primary Sources:

Kipling, Rudyard. *In Black and White*. India: Rupa Publications, 2012. Print.

---. *Under the Deodars*. India: Rupa Publications, 2012. Print.

---. *The Phantom Rickshaw and Other Eerie Tales*. India: Rupa Publications, 2010. Print.

---. *Kim*. India: Rupa Publications, 1999. Print.

---. *Plain Tales from the Hills*. India: Rupa Publications, 2012. Print.

---. *The Jungle Book*. New York: Barnes and Nobles Classics, 2012. Print.

---. *In the Rukh, 'Many Inventions'* . New York: House of Stratus. 2009. Print.

---. *Life's Handicap*. New York: Doubleday and McClure, 1899. Print.

---. *"If" Rewards and Fairies*. New York: Doubleday, Page and Co., 1910. 181-82. Print.

---."*Recessional*". Kipling: Poems. New York: Everyman's Library, 2007. 95. Print.

---. *"The White Man's Burden"*. McClure's 12 (Feb. 1899). Print.

---. *Something of Myself: For my Friends Known and Unknown*. Edinburgh: R & R Clark, 2006. Print.

Kipling, John Lockwood. *Beast and Man in India: A popular sketch of Indian Animals in Their Relations with the People*, London, Macmillan and Co, 1891. Print.

Secondary sources

Allen, Charles. *Kipling Sahib: India and the making of Rudyard Kipling*. London, Abacus,

2014. Print.

Castells, M. *The Power of Identity,* vol. II of *The Information Age: Economy, Society and Culture.* Oxford, Blackwell, 1997, Print.

Cody, David. *"Kipling's Imperialism".* The Victorian Web. N.p., 1988. Web. 5 Dec. 2015. <http://www.victorianweb.org/authors/kipling/r kimperialism.html>.

Du Bois, W.E.B. *The Souls of Black Folk.* New York: Gramercy Books, 1994.

Emerson, Ralph Waldo. *Essays* (First series). 1841. New York: Houghton Mifflin, 1876. Print.

Eril, Astrid. "*Rewriting as Re-Visioning: Modes of Representing the 'India Mutiny' in British Novels, 1857-2000.*" European Journal of English Studies 10.2 (2006). 163-85. Print.

Flood, Alison. "Rudyard Kipling admitted to plagiarism in jungle Book". *The Guardian* (London). Retrieved 18 December 2015.

Gilmour, David. *The Imperial Life of Rudyard Kipling.* Pimlico, 2003. Print.

Kumar ,Krishan, *The Making of English National Identity.* Cambridge: Cambridge UP, 2003. Print.

Lyotard, Jean-Francois. *The Postmodern Condition: A Report on Knowledge.* Trans. Geoff Bennington and Brian Massumi. 1979. Minneapolis: U. Of Minnesota P. 1984. Print.

Mandler, Peter. *The English National Character: The History of a Idea from Edmund Burke to Tony Blair.* New Haven: Yale UP, 2006. Print.

Metcalfe, Thomas. *The New Cambridge History of India. Vol. 3: Ideologies of the Raj.* Cambridge UP, 2003. Print

Meyers, Jeffrey. "Introduction" *Kim.* 1901. New York: Barnes and Nobles Classics, 2004. 15-29.

Mizelle, Brett. "Man Cannot Behold It Without Contemplating Himself": Monkeys, Apes and Human Identity in the Early American Republic." In *Explorations in Early American Culture,* by William Pencak and George W. Boudreau. [University Park, PA]: Pennsylvania Historical Association for the McNeil Center for Early

American Studies, 1998.

Newton, Michael. *Savage Girls and Wild Boys: A History of Feral Children.* Picador. 2004. Print.

Moore-Gilbert, Bart "*The Bhabhal of Tongues' reading Kipling, reading Bhabha*", *Writing India, 1757-1990: The Literature of British India.* Ed. Bart Moore-Gilbert. Manchester U P. 1996. 111-38. Print.

Nair, B Rukmini *"Lying on the Postcolonial Couch: The Idea of Indifference"*, University of Minnesota Press, Minneapolis, U.S.A, 2002. Print.

Nyman, Jopi. "Re-Reading Rudyard Kipling's 'English' Heroism: Narrating Nation in *The Jungle Book.*" in *Postcolonial Animal Tale from Kipling to Coetzee.* New Delhi: Atlantic Publishers and Distributors , 2003. 205-220. Orbis Litterarum. Web. 5 Dec. 2015. <http://onlinelibrary.wiley.com/doi/10.1034/j.16 00-0730.2001.d01-44.x/pdf>.

"Nobelprize.org". Nobelprize.org. Nobel media AB 2014.Web. 5 Aug. 2015. http://www.nobelprize.org/nobel_prizes/literatur e/laureates

http://www.kiplingsociety.co.uk
rg_speeches_17.html.Web 25 Aug 2015.

Orwell, George. *"Rudyard Kipling" 1946. Kipling's Mind and Art.* Ed. Andrew Rutherford. Stanford: Stanford U P. 1966. 70-84. Print.

Parry, Benita. *Delusions and Discoveries: Studies on India in the British Imagination,* 1880-1930. London : Allen Lane. 1972. Print.

Rao, K. Bhaskara. *Rudyard Kipling's India.* Norman: University of Oklahoma Press. 1967. Print.

Randall, Don. *"Post-Mutiny Allegories of Empire in Rudyard Kipling's Jungle Books."Texas Studies in Literature and Language. 41.1C* Spring (1998): 97-120 Rpt in Children's Literature Review, Ed. Scot Peacock.

Roy, Parama. *Indian Traffic: Identities in Question in Colonial and Postcolonial India.* Berkeley: U of California P, 1998. Print.

Said, Edward. *Culture and Imperialism* . 1993. New York: Knopf. 1994. Print.

---, *'Introduction'* Kipling, Rudyard. *Kim.* 1901. Ed. Edward Said. New York: Penguin, 1989. 7-46. Print.

---. *Orientalism.* 1978. New York: Vintage, 2003. Print.

Singh, Khushwant *Kipling's India:* India:Roli Publications Books Pvt. Ltd. 1994. Print.

Sullivan, Zohreh T. *Narratives of Empire: The Fiction of Rudyard Kipling.* Cambridge: Cambridge U P. 1993. Print.

Sandison, Alan. *"Kipling: The Artist and the Empire."* In *Kipling's Mind and Art.* Ed. Andrew Rutherford. 1964. Stanford: Stanford U P, 1966. 146-67. Print.

Trevelyan, G. M. *English Social History.* UK. Penguin Books UK, 1987. Print.

Tomlinson, J. *Globalisation and Culture.* Cambridge: Polity Press. 1999. Print.

Vishvanathan, Gauri. *Masks of Conquest: Literary Study and British Rule in India.* 1989.New York: Oxford UP, 1998. Print.

Wilson, Angus. *The Strange Ride of Rudyard Kipling.* Harmondsworth: Penguin. 1979. Print.

Wilson, Edmund, *"The Kipling that Nobody Read".* 1941. Kipling's Mind and Art. Ed. Andrew Rutherford. 1964. Stanford: Stanford UP, 1966. 17-69. Print.

From the same publisher.

Scandal: How homosexuality became a crime, by David Boyle

It was Saturday 6 April 1895. The weather was windy and drizzly as the passengers packed onto the quayside at Dover to catch the steam packet to Calais, due on the evening tide. Perhaps it was packed that night because of Easter the following week. Perhaps it wasn't as packed as some of the witnesses claimed later, or the downright gossips who weren't actually there. But it was still full. Those waiting on the quay wrapped up warm against the chilly Channel breeze and eyed each other nervously, afraid to meet anyone they knew, desperately wanting to remain anonymous.

Among those heading for France that night was an American, Henry Harland, the editor and co-founder of the notorious quarterly known as *The Yellow Book*, the journal of avant garde art and writing which had taken England by the scruff of the neck in the 1890s. Harland had come to Europe with his wife Aline, pretending to have been born in St Petersburg and planning to live in Paris, but had instead made his London flat, at 144 Cromwell Road, the very hive of excitement in the literary world. Henry James, Edmund Gosse 4 and Aubrey Beardsley came and went.

The parties were talked about with awe and excitement. Henry and Aline always spent the spring in Paris, so they were not leaving the country suddenly and in desperation, but it dawned on them that the reason the quayside was so packed that night was because many others were. The name of the ferry the Harlands boarded has been lost to history. It was probably the *Victoria* – her sister ship the Empress had been badly damaged in a collision the month before and was now in dry dock. There she heaved beside the sea wall, as the muffled passengers filed up the gangway, her twin rakish masts and her twin funnels belching smoke, her two paddlewheels poised to drive across the world's busiest sea lane at 18 knots, her stern flag flapping in the wind with the insignia of the London, Chatham and Dover Railway.

Harland had a good idea why the ferries were full, though he was still surprised. He was also aware of at least some of the implications for himself. Oscar Wilde had been arrested for 'gross indecency' that evening, having lost his libel action the day before. The news of the warrant for his arrest was in the evening papers, and included the information that Wilde had been arrested while he had been reading a copy of *The Yellow Book* (this was quite wrong, in fact; he was reading *Aphrodite* by Pierre Louys). Harland could only guess the motivations of those who were now suddenly crowding across the English Channel, but it looked remarkably like fear. They huddled in corners in the stateroom downstairs, out of the wind, damp and smuts, wondering perhaps whether they would ever see their native land again.

There was an unnerving atmosphere of menace that evening. One item in the evening papers implied that the nation was perched on the edge of a scandal that would make the establishment teeter. "If the rumours which are abroad tonight are proved to be correct we shall have such an exposure as has been unheard of in this country for many years past." Did it mean the exposure would reach those who run the nation, or did it mean something even more terrifying – that the exposure would spread downwards through society? As the passengers knew only too well, the combination of events which they had feared for a decade had now come to pass. It had been a few months short of ten years since the so-called 'Labouchère amendment' had been rushed through the House of Commons, criminalising homosexual activity of any kind between men. It was never quite clear why women were excluded – there is no evidence for the old story that Queen Victoria claimed it was impossible.

For ten years now, they had watched the rising sense of outrage at the very idea of 'homosexuality' – though the term was not yet in common use – and had realised that there might come a time when that law was enforced with an unsurpassed ferocity. It wasn't that they necessarily had anything to be ashamed of – quite the reverse – but they had reputations to be lived down, some event in their past or some 'unfortunate' relationship behind them.

Now that public concern had turned to what looked like public hysteria, they clearly had to be vigilant. They did not want to be accused, as Oscar Wilde was accused, by a violent aristocrat of doubtful sanity, and would then have to respond in the courts or the press. They could not face the fatal knock on the front door from a smiling acquaintance who would turn out to be a dangerous blackmailer. But now the unthinkable had happened. Wilde had been stupid enough to sue the Marquess of Queensberry for libel, and had lost. The public had driven each other into a crescendo of rage and it seemed only sensible to lie low in Paris for a while. Or Nice or Dieppe, or the place where the British tended to go in flight from the law – Madrid. Anywhere they could be beyond the reach of the British legal system.

As we shall see, one of those who fled, as I discovered during the research that led to this book, was my own great-great-grandfather – escaping for the second time in a just over a decade, in a story that my own family had suppressed for three generations.

*

It is no small matter to flee your home and go

abroad, especially to do so within the space of a few hours to gather your belongings and make arrangements for your property or your money. As it is, escape was only a solution available to those wealthy enough to flee. It is even tougher perhaps for those in some kind of unconventional relationship, ambiguous to the outside world – but perhaps not ambiguous enough – aware that the decision to go was probably irreversible. It might look like an admission of guilt.

On the other hand, what might happen when the newspapers could unleash this kind of bile? What would happen when they had successfully gaoled Wilde with hard labour and turned on his friends, and anyone else who looked unusual? What would happen if the rumours were correct and the scandal would shortly engulf the government and royal family? Harland did not know at this stage that, when the news about *The Yellow Book* became clear on Monday morning, a mob would gather outside the offices of his publishers Bodley Head, and would break all the windows. "It killed The Yellow Book and it nearly killed me," said publisher John Lane later.

We know now that, in the event, the threatened

conflagration did not take place, but in the remaining 72 years while Section 11 of the Criminal Law Amendment Act, the Labouchère Amendment, stayed on the statute books, 75,000 were prosecuted under its terms, among them John Gielgud, Lord Montagu and Alan Turing. Many thousands of lives were ruined – Turing committed suicide not long afterwards, having been forced to undergo hormone treatment that made him grow breasts. Yet that moment of fear in Britain in 1895, unprecedented in modern times, has been largely forgotten. It is remembered as a sniggering remnant of gossip, about the number of English aristocrats or others in public life, living incognito in Dieppe, or glimpsed in the bars in Paris, and the awareness as a result that they had something to hide.

One of the purposes of this book is to remember it for what it was – one of the most disturbing chapters in modern English history, when public horror at sexual behaviour reached such intensity that nobody seemed completely safe, and nobody could be relied on to protect you. And when a man like Wilde, the darling of the theatre critics, with two sell-out shows in London's

West End theatres, could be brought low by a furious, litigious pugilist – well, really, who was safe?

This unique moment of fear in English history came at a peculiar moment, at perhaps the apogee of tolerance in so many other ways – women were cycling and getting university degrees, training to be doctors. Mohandas Gandhi was a London-trained barrister working in South Africa. George Bernard Shaw was overturning assumptions about the right way to dress, eat and spell. H. G. Wells was sleeping his way through the ranks of the young female Fabians. Edward Carpenter, in his sandals, was advertising freedom from the constraints of conventional sexuality, having forged a gay relationship with a working class man from Sheffield. William Morris was still, just, preaching a revolution based on medieval arts and crafts. And yet the rage at the idea that men should love each other sexually threatened to overwhelm everything. That morning, Queensberry had received a telegram from an anonymous supporter, which read: "Every man in the City is with you. Kill the bugger."

Why did it happen? Partly because of growing

public concern following the Labouchère amendment, sneaked though Parliament in 1885, but even that was more than the individual brainchild of a lone radical. Why this shift from tolerance of the changing role of women and emerging new ideas to this threatening public rage? How did homosexuality emerge as a key issue in English public life? The answer lies in the events that took place in Dublin a decade before, starting with the political aftermath of the murder of Lord Frederick Cavendish, the son of the Duke of Devonshire and the newly-appointed Chief Secretary to Ireland.

*

But I had a more personal reason for finding out the answers to some of these questions. My family lived in Dublin in the 1880s. The reason that they don't any more, and that I was born in England not Ireland, was because of those same events there in that decade. Until the last few years, when I began researching this book, I was unaware of them. All I knew was that my great-great-grandfather, the banker Richard Boyle, had left

Dublin suddenly and under a cloud around 1884. His photograph has been torn out of the family photo album, with only his forehead remaining. There are no likenesses of him anywhere that I know about. The letters related to these events in the family, and what followed, have long since been destroyed. I believe I was even there when my grandfather burned the last of them on the bonfire around 1975.

I had always been interested in what might have happened, but had assumed that the memories were now beyond recovery, just as the fate of my great-great-grandfather was lost in the mists of unfathomable time. As it turned out, I was wrong. I was working on another incident in Irish history in the British Library, and discovered as I did so that a whole raft of Victorian Irish newspapers had been digitised and were now searchable online. On an impulse, I put in the name 'Richard Boyle' and searched through the references in the Dublin papers. Then, suddenly, my heart began beating a little faster, because there it was – the first clue I found to a personal tragedy, and a national tragedy too: this was the spark that lit the fuse which led to the criminalisation of gay behaviour and the great moment of fear that followed the arrest of Oscar Wilde. That first clue led to others, which led to others. I will never know the whole story, but what I did discover took me on a historical rollercoaster, and an emotional one, which catapulted me back to the strangely familiar world of the end of the nineteenth century – and a glimpse of that sudden fear in April 1895 that drove many of those affected so suddenly abroad...

From: Scandal: How Homosexuality Became a Crime, David Boyle, The Real Press, 2016

www.therealpress.co.uk